A House for Sergin

Hilda Perera
Illustrated by Leyla Torres

Rigby

© 1999 by Rigby

a division of Reed Elsevier Inc.
500 Coventry Lane
Crystal Lake, IL 60014

Executive Editor: Lynelle H. Morgenthaler
Senior Designer: Lucy Smith

04 03 02 01 00 99
10 9 8 7 6 5 4 3

Printed in Singapore

ISBN 0-7635-5709-9

Sergín was a bright, good Cuban boy. He liked to do
the same things other boys his age liked to do, but he
needed a wheelchair to get around.

3

Because Sergín liked animals, his parents let him have all the pets he wanted. He had a big dog, a small cat, a little white rabbit, and a chatty parrot that called him Sergín. Sergín would wake up early to feed them and play with them before he went to school. Then he would practice the trumpet that his mom bought him.

In the afternoon, Sergín liked to play dominoes. Some of his papa's friends would come to the house to play with Sergín and his father. Every day Sergín kept so busy that he didn't have time to think about how he couldn't walk or run like the other children. More than anything, though, his busy life made him forget about how afraid he had been when he came from Cuba in a small boat.

The only thing he had to complain about was that their house was too small. His father, Don Manuel, understood, but he didn't earn enough money to allow them to rent a bigger one. "We need more money, Sergín," he said to his son. And that is how Sergín had the idea to help his mother with the bakery business she had started when they came from Cuba.

First she started out by making toasted meringues that sold for twenty cents apiece. Later, she got a recipe for chocolate cupcakes, and Sergín stirred the batter all by himself. After that, she learned to make cakes and pies, and little by little her business grew. Sergín made sure that everything was very clean and neat, and he got to know all the people who bought baked goods from him by name.

Soon they were making a lot of money. Sergín asked his father, "Papa, do you think we can look for a bigger house now?"

In fact, Sergín's mom and dad looked in the area and came across a big, old house for low rent.

"Oh, good!" said Sergín's mother, Doña María.

But his father immediately had some concerns, "It's a very old house. We'd have to make a lot of repairs."

Sergín's mother kept thinking about the matter. *Who could help us?* she wondered.

Right away, she thought of Don Lucas, the carpenter who came to play dominoes with Sergín and his father.

"Listen, Don Lucas," she told him, "we have found a magnificent, big house for Sergín, but it's very old and needs a lot of repairs."

"Well, Doña María, as far as I'm concerned, it's no sooner said than done. I'll also make the doorways extra wide so that he doesn't hurt his arms when he goes through them."

Sergín's mom felt very happy, and she wondered who could help do the bricklaying.

Right away, his father thought of Don Fernando, his bricklayer friend who came to play dominoes. He said to him, "Oh, Don Fernando, we have found a magnificent, big house for Sergín, but it needs a lot of repairs. Who could help us?"

"I could, Don Manuel. As far as I'm concerned, the work is as good as done. Instead of front steps, I'll make a little ramp that's not too steep so that Sergín can go down it easily."

Who could do the plumbing? wondered Sergín's parents.

Right away, they thought of Don Pedro, the plumber who came to play dominoes. Doña María said, "Don Pedro, we have found a magnificent house for Sergín, but it needs a lot of repairs."

"Not to worry, Doña María. Tell me what needs to be done, and it will be my pleasure to do it. I'll build a special shower so that Sergín can fit inside it in his wheelchair."

"What about the electricity?" asked Sergín's father.

"Of course, I'll take care of that," said Don Justo, who also played dominoes with them. "I'll install buzzers in every room of the house so Sergín can call for you easily."

Doña María was still thinking, *We already have a carpenter, a bricklayer, a plumber, and an electrician. But who can fix up the yard with all those shrubs in it?*

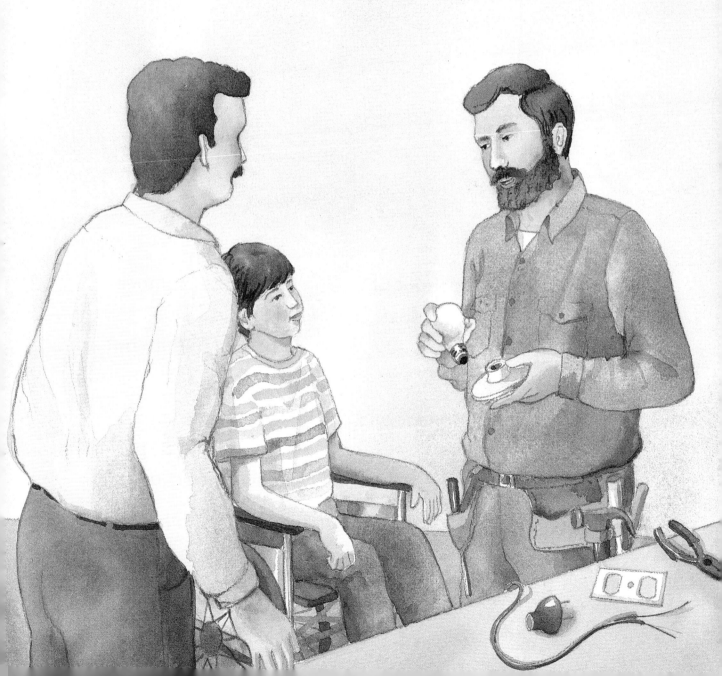

Then Sergín remembered that Don Juan, who also came to play in the afternoons, was a gardener.

Sergín's father waited for him. He said, "Don Juan, we have found a magnificent house for Sergín, but it has a huge yard. We can't do anything until the shrubs are cut down."

"Well, you can get started because I'll cut them down, Don Manuel. I'm going to plant a lot of flowers so that Sergín can see them every time he looks out a window."

13

"That's great!" said Sergín and his parents. As usual when something good happened, Sergín went to his room to play "Guantanamera," his favorite Cuban song, on the trumpet.

The repair work started right away. The shrubs that covered everything were cut down, the walls were fixed, big picture windows were put in, and the plumbing and electricity were repaired. It was starting to look like new.

When it came time to paint, Sergín's father said, "That's my job." And he went to buy paint and paintbrushes. In only three days, he painted everything.

15

La Cubana
Fine Baked Goods

"Now we can move!" exclaimed Sergín, happy that everything was ready. He put the rabbit and the little cat in boxes, fastened the parrot's cage, and put the leash on the dog.

The day they moved was a big treat. Sergín rushed around in his wheelchair and went through the wide doorways without banging his arms. His mother sang the whole time, and his father could not stop smiling.

They set up the bakery business in the front room and put up a sign that read: "La Cubana. Fine Baked Goods." There they fit all the counters made of white wood and shiny glass that Sergín's father had ordered. It looked like a very elegant place.

One afternoon, when they were in a big hurry, Sergín was mixing cake batter at full speed. Suddenly he bumped his chair, and the bowl of batter fell to the floor.

Sergín couldn't hold back the tears that rolled down his cheeks. "You see, Mom? I can't do anything right with these legs of mine."

"I will not let you say things like that!" said his mother. "People can do whatever they want if they set their minds to it. I want you to know that there was a president who used a wheelchair. His name was Franklin Delano Roosevelt. So it's not for me to say whether you can mix the cake batter or not. It all depends on what you set your mind to do. Look, we'll clean all this up, and you can start again. You'll see, you'll do it right this time!"

In fact, Sergín finished the cake, and it turned out just right.

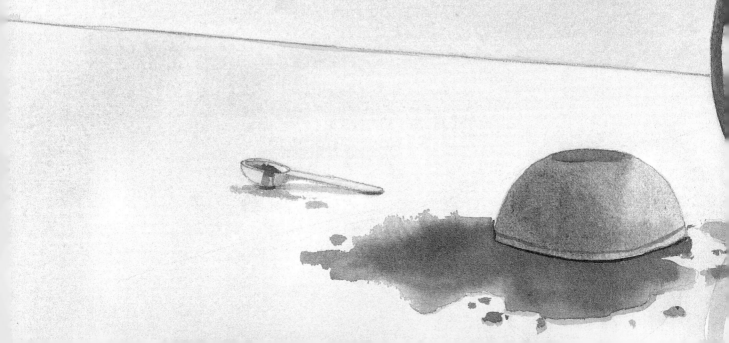

The next morning, Sergín got up very early, took care of his animals, and was ready to go to school at seven o'clock sharp. A special van came to pick him up.

His mom was afraid that the other children would laugh at him when they saw him get out at the school. In fact, there were some who couldn't keep from snickering. But Sergín ignored them. He simply said hello and headed for his class.

Sergín was so determined and paid such careful attention that, in a few days, he was the best one at reading. He also practiced writing until he could do it perfectly. When the class played basketball during gym, Sergín was the referee, and everyone agreed his calls were fair.

The day of the school's anniversary parade was quickly drawing near. Some girls were going to do ballet steps. Other students were going to march with flags and wear important-looking uniforms.

Sergín was dying to join in, but he didn't know how.

At last the idea came to him. He would play the trumpet. But how, if he couldn't walk?

"If your teacher says it's okay, I'll take you," his mother told him.

Sergín was so happy that he did what he always did when something good happened. He played "Guantanamera" on his trumpet!

The teacher said yes. On parade day, it was a big surprise for everyone when Sergín played the trumpet in his wheelchair as his mother pushed him along.

"Hooray for Sergín!" shouted the crowd. "Hip, hip, hooray!"

Sergín felt like the happiest boy in the world. Since that day, every time the school had a game, Sergín got to announce the start with the toot-toot of his trumpet.

And he became the most popular boy in school.